Changing Lens: A Teen's Journey Across Five Languages

Felix Mao

Bridge21 | Alhambra, CA

Changing Lens: A Teen's Journey Across Five Languages
by Felix Mao

Published by Bridge21 Publications, LLC

Distributed by Casemate Group
Casemate Academic: USA and North America
Script Publisher Services: UK, Europe, and the Rest of the World

Illustration by Felix Mao and Irena Mao.

Published in the United States of America

ISBN 978-1-62643-119-5 Paperback
ISBN 978-1-62643-120-1 ePub | ebook pdf | Kindle

Contents

Introduction

It was September 5th, 2023, a sweltering Tuesday. I walked into the Pinkham building, my first day as a high school freshman. There was something special about returning to school. Maybe it was seeing the friends I played soccer with every day, rain or shine. Maybe it was the new classes and teams I would be part of. More than anything, I just enjoyed being back.

This year felt even more special—the start of a new chapter, high school. When I took my first steps into school that day, I looked forward to every moment. I knew I would learn, grow, and be challenged in ways that I couldn't yet imagine and that excited me the most. The thought of embarking on this journey alongside my peers made it even better. Together, we would go through the ups and downs of high school, and create memories that would last a lifetime, even if we eventually went our own ways. Amid the chaos of that first day—the crowded hallways, new teachers, unfamiliar faces—I couldn't help but feel a surge of excitement for the adventures ahead.

Later that day, I sat in history class. My last history class had been boring, and the sweltering classroom—infused with a weird tea-like smell—didn't help. But those experiences were quickly shattered. On the screen flashed a question:

What makes the human species special?

At first, we were confused. Humans are different from other animals, but they aren't that special—right? The best answer we came up with was that humans were smarter, the dominant species. That wasn't wrong, but our teacher introduced a different idea:

Language.

Humans, he explained, have precise language systems that allow us to communicate effectively, and also connect with the world around us.

This answer stayed with me after the class ended. I began to realize how important language is to our species. It wasn't merely a tool like a pickaxe or a hammer, nor just a means of communication;

it was something far more significant. It allows humans to share ideas across generations, from the earliest cave paintings to the digital age of smartphones and the internet.

Language felt like a bridge and a doorway for me, connecting us around and opening pathways to the world. From English to Chinese, Arabic to Swahili, Greek to Latin, every word, character, and phrase allows us to communicate with others, so we can share happy moments with families, explore the world, and even simply say hello to a stranger at the park.

This belief sparked my passion for language. I chose to learn not one, not two, but five languages: English (technically), Chinese, Spanish, Latin, and Japanese. Even saying that still feels overwhelming. To this day, I am still not entirely sure how I managed it. Yet here I am, slowly becoming a language enthusiast—or, more formally, a polyglot. From using Duolingo every day and keeping a digital bird happy to struggling with Latin participles, I have found both challenges and joy in learning, especially learning a variety of them at the same time. With each one, I discovered something new, and they have led me on journeys that would never have crossed my mind in a million dreams.

My Story

One language sets you in a corridor for life. Two languages open every door along the way.

—Frank Smith

You might be wondering: Why did you put yourself through all that pain and suffering? Why did you bother learning five languages? Isn't learning a language a pain?

Well, why do people learn languages in the first place? To many, the answer is simple: I want to talk with more people. And that's what I originally thought, too.

Before I begin my journey of language learning, we will need to go back to when I was a child and explore the concept of discovery. When I was a preschooler, I lived in a small room in an apartment in Newport, Jersey City. At that early point in my life, I only knew the small courtyard in front of the building, where we would ice skate in the winter and play soccer in the summer, the playgrounds across the street, where my grandpa took me to play on the swings, and my preschool, which I dreaded going to because of nap-time. To me, that was my world. Frankly, I hadn't seen any other part of the almost 200 million square miles of Earth.

However, I would soon discover that Jersey City was only a fraction of the outside world, a needle in the haystack. The first time I made the journey across the Hudson River, through the Lincoln Tunnel to New York City, to say I was stunned would be a complete understatement. It looked and felt like a whole new world. I saw buildings to my left and right shooting into the sky, some made of concrete and some of glass; cars of all types zooming left and right—red, yellow, black, minivans, trucks, motorcycles, you name it—and lots and lots of people. I never realized that the world had so many people in it. I remember walking on 5th Avenue and seeing the grand Empire State Building high over my head, seemingly touching the stars I read about in my children's books. I remember going to Chinatown, a part of the city that felt completely different from the rest. I remember driving into Times Square at night, which felt completely different from the city during daytime. I also remember taking the ferry to Staten Island and asking myself, how can the world be so

big? It was nothing like the quaint park at the foot of my apartment building. It was the real world, the world outside my tiny bubble.

That moment changed how I saw the world.

After going home to Newport, I would beg my parents to take me to other places. I had had such a good impression of elsewhere. My little world was no longer just the playground and the courtyard but also the lights on the buildings and the sounds of the cars. After

experiencing a new city for the first time, and being introduced to a new culture, I was curious to find out what the rest of the world looked like. I wanted to discover. I wanted to be amazed like I was when I first saw New York.

So, I pulled up a world map and found myself completely in awe. Names like Germany, China, and India floated through my brain. New York was just a teeny tiny little speck. In fact, Jersey City was so small that apparently the map makers didn't even think it was necessary to include it on maps. Thanks to the trip to New York and my curiosity, though, I now understood that the world wasn't just Newport, or even the United States. There were another 195 countries out there! At that point, I became determined—Was the whole world the same? Was it different? What was the world like? I would soon find out.

Fast forward a couple months, and a five-year-old me was twisting and turning in my bed, so excited that I couldn't fall asleep. Why? Well, my parents had decided that we would be flying to China to visit friends and family. A fun trip, something that would keep me entertained for at least part of a boring summer? It was enough for five-year-old me to move around all night, getting only an hour of sleep before I was forcefully removed from my bed at three in the morning to go to Newark Airport. During the flight, I couldn't help but wonder what Shanghai would be like. Would it be like New York?

As we descended into Shanghai, once again my mind was completely blown. Just seeing the city of Shanghai, halfway across the world, was mind-blowing—and it was completely different from the apartments of Jersey City and the skyscrapers of New York. Instead of skyscrapers and cars, there were small houses and various kinds of skyscrapers. Still modern but a unique type of modernity. There were still crowds of people and cars, but I could tell that they were unlike the people and cars I knew in America. It was obvious that this city had a completely distinct vibe. At that point, I told myself: The world isn't just New York. It's full of cities, vastly different cities, each one with a unique journey waiting to be unfolded.

But something felt off. This trip felt different from the first time I visited New York City. China felt much more foreign. It wasn't just the distance, though one city was twenty miles away from my house and the other one was almost four hundred times further. There was something else that made my first experiences in these two cities completely different.

The difference was language, and it mattered more than I expected.

That difference stayed with me. After coming back from China, I couldn't shake the feeling of confusion. I grew up in a Chinese household, and my parents immigrated to America from there. Yet when I went to China I couldn't say a simple greeting, much less receive a gift, because I didn't understand how to read, write, or speak the language. When I met my numerous grandparents, cousins, aunts, and uncles for the first time, they enthusiastically walked right up to me, saying all kinds of hellos, praises, and more. They treated me as if I were their son, and I truly felt grateful. When they gave me gifts, I wanted to respond; I wanted to say something to match the enthusiasm they showed me, even if it was only something simple, but

all I could muster was a simple 你好 (ni hao → hello) and 谢谢 (xie xie → thank you). It would be like that for almost all of the trip. Don't get me wrong, the trip was great, and being able to experience China was better than anything I could have asked for, but the language barrier caused me to feel distanced from the people and the culture around me. Part of me wanted to blame this on anxiety about meeting people, but deep down I knew that it was because I didn't speak Chinese well.

So, when I got home from that trip, I told my parents that I wanted to learn Chinese. The next time I went to China, I wanted to be able to connect with those people and understand the wonderful culture that China has to offer. Not being able to have a conversation in Chinese would definitely prevent that.

I desired to learn a second language because I wanted to feel included and experience that sense of immersion in a foreign land.

That was when everything shifted.

That trip to China also taught me something else about this world: Unlike what I originally thought as a child, everywhere in the world has its own culture. I wondered: how many unique cultures were there in the world? Growing up, I was always a curious kid. This curiosity, especially my interests in discovering new cultures, let me develop a love for traveling, as traveling meant exploring new places and discovering new traditions, cuisines, architecture, landmarks, and more. However, just because a place had the food, the landmarks, and the people didn't mean I could fully enjoy it. As a tourist, you can take photos and experience a little bit of local streets, but I wanted more. Learning their language felt like the first step. As Federico Fellini says, "a different language is a different vision of life."

This feeling stayed with me and motivated me to keep going on the journey. Two years later, when my family planned a trip to Cancun in second grade, I decided to start Spanish classes at school. Sure, I could admire the Mayan pyramids, the resort beaches, and the food without speaking Spanish, but I wanted more than admiration. I

wanted to understand, to immerse myself, and to see Mexico through the lens of its own language. That drive—to engage more fully with the cultures I encounter—kept me studying Spanish through high school, knowing it could open doors to many countries beyond Mexico.

Then, it was Latin. But it was the culture that interested me enough to take the language, given Latin is a dead language. I fell in love with Greek and Roman mythology after reading the Percy Jackson & the Olympians series and doing a project on the Greek gods. In middle school, this series was my favorite, and I probably read each book from both the Olympians and Heroes of Olympus series at least ten times. Because of that, Latin might be interesting and worth a shot. At least, Latin could teach me a lot more about the Greek and Roman myths. Additionally, going back to the more academic side, of the languages I learned, Latin has probably been the most beneficial. As the "father" of Romance languages, Latin made learning other languages like Spanish and English easier, as these languages shared many things in common, like prefixes and suffixes, words with similar meanings, and more. Latin didn't just teach me vocabulary, beneficial for other classes, it changed how I understand language.

Finally, there was Japanese. This was long after my first trips to Mexico and China, but that same motivation stuck with me. When my family announced that we would be going to Japan in ninth grade, to say I was happy would be an understatement. Going to Japan was a dream come true for me, and something I had been begging my parents for years. First, Japanese food was simply better than anything else. From ramen to sushi to sashimi, even a small food stand on the street would probably be better than some restaurants in the United States. Second, Japanese culture was one of a kind, and something that I very much enjoyed. From samurais to anime, Japanese culture was one of the most diverse and unique cultures in the world. I wanted to understand and appreciate it, just like with Mexican culture. Finally, the city of Tokyo was a futuristic and beautiful city. The neon lights and modern buildings on every corner, along with the most random but useful gadgets that you could imagine, made the city of Tokyo

seem like life in the future.

However, learning from past experience, I knew that if I really wanted to accomplish all the goals and dreams I had for Japan, I would need to first learn the language itself. As with any other country, I didn't want to just visit Japan—I wanted to understand it. Thus, I started to study Japanese on my own. Using the online language app Duolingo, I started to learn the Japanese words and characters which would allow me to navigate the streets of Tokyo—hopefully.

My motivation for learning all these languages came down to immersion and discovery. Whether it was that I needed language skills to function, or learning a language felt like unlocking a new dimension—I felt motivated. And the feeling hasn't faded. There were times on the journey where I got bored, felt let down, or was sick of it, but in the end, these languages built character, and the end result definitely made up for any struggle I faced. So now, let me take you on my journey, a path full of ups, downs, laughs, tears, and everything in between.

My Journey

Knowledge of languages is the doorway to wisdom.

— Roger Bacon

Learning a single language is no small feat. From grammar to vocabulary to pronunciation, a language presents many challenges, making the process of learning a language, to put it in simple words, at times quite miserable. But with those challenges come rich stories, cultural depth, and unexpected joys. For example, the process of learning Spanish isn't just about conjugations and verb tenses, but also about traditional Spanish foods like paella, Spanish dances like La Cumbia, and so much more. Latin isn't just ancient texts—it also tells the stories of the myths of the gods and heroes that shaped civilizations. Learning a language is hard, and in the process it's not every day that something unique and interesting happens. But something has encouraged me to learn the languages I did. As boring as learning a language can be, there will always be something fascinating about it. Each day, no matter if I am walking into a Spanish classroom, a Latin classroom, an online Japanese course, or going to Chinese school, I know that maybe I will learn something cool. And that motivates me to keep learning—and when something cool happens, like performing traditional art or visiting a country, it makes the (painful) process seem completely worth it. I would like to share my experiences learning not one, not two, but five languages, including challenges faced, breakthroughs, and, most importantly, the fun I had along the way.

English

A new language is a new life.

— *Anonymous*

I know what you're thinking: Why are you including English? You're probably right, there really isn't a point. Why include English in this book? I grew up in America, and it isn't a foreign language to me. However, I think it is still important to include my own story about learning English for a couple of reasons.

First of all, English was the first language I learned. "But you grew up in America, that doesn't count!" Well, technically, it does count as my first language. People tend to overlook their native language as it's not "foreign" language, but it is still a language.

For someone that grew up in America, the English language comes naturally to them, as if they knew how to speak it right when they were born. But this isn't the case for everyone.

For example, my grandparents. They grew up in China, and immigrated to the United States without having learned much English.

It wasn't their first language—that was Chinese. Thus, it was quite hard for them to get accustomed to the language, as common and easy as it seems to us. I remember that, every day, Grandpa would use Duolingo to learn English—and he still couldn't pass the first-grade level. He constantly asked me: Felix, what is this in Chinese? So, as unimportant as you think your first language is, remember that it was where you began, and as easy as it might seem to you, it is still a foreign language to some others.

More importantly, however, the English language is what enabled me to embark on my journey of language learning. For one, it has allowed me to be able to gain information and accumulate knowledge. Just think about it—where would we be if we didn't know how English worked? I could write a grammatically incorrect sentence that sounds horrible—something unclear and repetitive—and I wouldn't even know it. That's if I never learned basic English grammar.

Secondly, English has many parallels in other languages. The English word corpus is something that has continuously evolved and adapted, absorbing influences from various cultures and languages as they each came into contact with America, enriching its vocabulary and expressions. For example, the English word "ketchup" originates from Chinese, believe it or not, and the word "cartoon" is from Italy. Does that mean Mickey Mouse is Italian? Thus, while it may seem mundane to some, understanding and mastering English opens doors to a vast and diverse culture—similar to that of Spanish or Chinese—it's just that we overlook its culture given we are all fluent at the language. So, even though English is something that we just know by default, it definitely counts as a language that is learned.

I myself started to learn English as soon as I could speak words, like every other American child. I went to preschool, then kindergarten, then the first grade. There, I learned how to say certain words, I learned my ABCs, and I learned how to read and write, all the basic stuff I needed to communicate with others, instead of a mixture of goo goo gaa gaa, screaming, and pointing. This all seems pretty normal when it comes to learning a language. Ironically though, I struggled a lot more learning those elements for the first time in English rather than in Spanish, even though I grew up in America. That's probably because English was my first language, and, obviously, learning new things, especially at that age, is tough.

Eventually, near the end of third grade, I had the basics of English figured out. I had learned basic sentence structure, some basic grammar

including syntax and conjugations, and a lot of vocabulary. I learned that each sentence needs a subject and a verb, and adjectives like "pretty" or "big" go with nouns, to describe them. I also practiced writing—lots of practice—both willingly and unwillingly. At school, I was assigned to write in a journal, to talk about what I did on the weekend or what I ate the day before. Every time I would pick up a pencil and scribble three or four simple sentences, like "I met a big dog," in very big handwriting, sometimes even all capital letters, then raised my hand and screamed "I'm done!" so that I could go outside. Now, obviously, this was kindergarten-me (imagine if this book was written like that!). As I got older, and became a third, fourth, and fifth grader, my writing got better. By the end of the fifth grade, I could write a decently complex essay or lab report. Now, words like "big" and "pretty" might get repeated ten or more times, but the fact that I could use words like photosynthesis and electromagnetism made up for it. Right?

Although throughout elementary school I found some parts of the learning process annoying and boring, I was succeeding—and that was very satisfying. Every time we had an English quiz, I made sure I was prepared. And every time I got a score of 100 I would be extremely happy—not because of the grade, but because I'd get a Starburst or a Jolly Rancher.

It was the same for projects. Whether it was the chicken- and duck-hatching lab in second grade, the maglev train lab in third grade, or the capstone project in fifth grade, I completed each with relative ease. My writing and grammar may not have been the best, but it got the message across, and it was good enough to impress the teachers.

Occasionally, I did run into some trouble. One time, in fourth grade, I was tasked with writing a play regarding the American Revolution, and for once I struggled. I spent hours thinking of the right words to use, but all that ever came to mind was "taxation without representation," not the adjectives or verbs that I needed. In the end, the play ended up being a random jumble of words (my public speaking skills did not help) that barely got a passable grade. But all in all, those struggles happened at most three or four times in elementary school, and most of my English learning journey to that point felt quite easy. I was basically practicing English constantly, just like everyone else, and to anyone that has tried learning a language, they know that consistency and practice are the key to fluency. At that moment, I considered my English fluent, and I had learned all I needed to know.

That soon changed, however. During Covid, I transferred to Rye Country Day School. I wasn't expecting that much of a difference and only knew that their humanities program was a lot better than my elementary school's. They probably knew more vocabulary than I did, put on more plays, and read more interesting books—but I believed that I'd still definitely go right into sixth grade without any issues.

I was wrong.

I walked into my first English class, expecting to ace the class.

Immediately, though, I knew something was different. The warm and supportive smile of my elementary school teacher was replaced by the stern look of an older and stricter teacher, the type of gaze that showed she understood you didn't want to be there.

I was assigned to a seat next to another new kid, and while we were introducing ourselves to each other, a loud scream pierced my eardrum! "Don't talk in my class!"

The next forty or so minutes felt like forty or so years. Not only did our teacher's presence make the class seem so much worse than it was—I was completely lost as to the information. The terms "subordinate pronoun" and "preposition" floated through my head, and not one did I recognize. I remember walking out of that class and saying to the kid next to me: "What in the world was that?"

I later found that, to my surprise, my grammar and English foundation were terrible. The kids who had been there for a couple of years not only had done much more of the stuff I mentioned above, but their prior English teachers had laid a much better language foundation for the students than I had at my previous school, whether in terms of grammar, vocabulary, or just knowledge of the English curriculum.

As a week went by, I found that English class—once such a walk in the park—had become a real challenge. I knew nothing about the grammar I was being taught, and not much else made sense, either. That was when I realized that, as "simple" of a language as English is, there is so much more that I needed to learn to consider myself to have mastered English. What elementary school taught me was just the tip of the iceberg. Under the water there were so much more.

As sixth grade went on, I knew that I needed to do something. My grades were average at best, which had never happened to me before in English. Most days I felt lost. In contrast to other classes, like history and math, where I enjoyed the material and was doing well, it was quite the opposite in English. While the teaching might not have been that strong—I had much better math and history teachers—I also hadn't built enough of a foundation to understand what we were studying in sixth grade.

I was trying to figure it all out myself, which, looking back, was one of the worst decisions I could have made. Every time you learn something new, regardless of the topic, you will struggle—even if it's something you've been practicing for your whole life. What I should have done was to find help and support, whether through a tutor, my parents, or even finding my teacher during free time—but I was too stubborn, and tried solving every problem myself. This didn't end well. As the year went on, and the material got harder, I went from barely understanding and keeping up to being one of the worst students in the class. My thoughts swirled around me. Was this word a preposition or a conjunction? Why was "who" used here, not "whom"? Why was this capitalized and that wasn't?

That January, my parents saw my report card—with a B+ glaring out. Over dinner, my mom asked: "Felix, what's happening in English? You never get grades this bad!"

After some arguing and a few headaches, we came up with a plan. Every night, my family and I would practice grammar. We practiced direct objects, indirect objects, commas, capitalization, and every aspect of the class for hours every day. My sister might have been asleep, and I might have been yawning, but my mom pushed me to keep studying. On Saturdays, when all my friends were outside playing sports, my dad pushed me to study for my tests. To say it was annoying is an understatement. Every day, I saw the people around me spend less effort and get better results. I felt like my good results would never come.

But I persevered (with some help from my parents) and eventually those good results did come. My English got better, and so did my grades. And from then on, it was basically smooth sailing (but for real).

I never really struggled with grammar again, as I had built a solid foundation thanks to that arduous sixth-grade ELA class. In seventh and eighth grades, whenever we went over the aspects of grammar—like participles, objects, who and whom—it felt easy, and I usually got grades of 100. When I got to high school, I didn't even have to worry about all that grammar, it just seemed to come naturally.

Writing, though—that was a whole different story. When I first went to school, I especially hated writing. I loathed essays the most (maybe because of the daily journal entries I had to write) and, to be quite honest, I was terrible at it. I saw myself as a STEM student and believed I was destined to study math or science—not because of how good I was at those subjects but because of how bad I was at writing. In the sixth grade, with all my grammar struggles, my writing was horrendous too. However, after two years, as I continued studying English and other subjects, I came to enjoy writing—not out of force but out of curiosity. The more I wrote, the more confidence I gained, and each essay, each journal entry, and each paragraph that I wrote improved. I began to embrace the idea that I wasn't just a STEM kid—I was also a writer, and I had a passion for improving my writing. The failures I experienced in sixth and seventh grades turned into growth and development as soon as I entered high school.

As soon as I wasn't stressing about grammar, I was able to fully appreciate English not just as a curriculum but as a language. All those years I had treated English as a class and failed to recognize it for what it truly was: a language. As I delved deeper into English, the complexity and richness of the language extended far beyond what I had initially perceived. It wasn't merely about mastering vocabulary and syntax but understanding the cultural connotations embedded within the language. Moreover, as I encountered more diverse literature and engaged in deeper discussions, I came to appreciate the depth that English offered. It enriched my intellectual and emotional understanding of the world around me in ways that I wouldn't have known if I had only treated it as a class and not a language. Thus, what began as a simple journey of learning a language became something much bigger.

As I moved through my school's English curriculum, I discovered unique and fun parts of the language, notably through the books we read in class. We read classics like *Romeo and Juliet* and *Macbeth*, fiction like *The Giver* by Lois Lowry, and non-fiction like *The Line Becomes A River*. Now, after reading so much, and understanding the language through so many angles and lenses, this once boring and mundane language has become a vivid one. My exposure to a wide variety of English literature, from works in

Old English to modern texts, opened my eyes to the beauty of the language. Now, as a teenager, though I read less fiction stories (and if I do it's fantasy adventure like *Harry Potter*), I still find interest in the nuances of the language itself. The metaphors, similes, and vivid imagery that many authors and poets use to bring stories to life helped bring color and excitement into English for me.

Now, I can safely say, I have good command of English. The journey of learning English wasn't as boring as I thought it was, even if it was very mundane compared to other languages. I learned that English is just like any other language, and it should be treated as one. Before, I always thought that English was just a class, made up of reading, writing, speaking, and grammar. However, after going to a new school with a stronger program, I began to see much more in it.

English stopped feeling like a class but started feeling like a language.

Chinese

一个新的语言是一个新的生命

— *Anonymous*

Finally, an actual foreign language. Well, kind of. Being from a bilingual family, the Chinese language also came way more naturally for me than, say, Spanish or Latin. I lived in a Chinese speaking environment and had always heard bits and pieces of the language. However, that didn't necessarily translate to the learning process being easy. In reality, it was actually quite painful, even for bilingual people like me. I know many people who, despite being Chinese, aren't actually that good at Chinese. In fact, many American-born Chinese (ABC) teenagers, shockingly, don't even know Chinese. But why?

Well, to many people, even second gens, Chinese is considered a hard language to learn, and the process is often seen by many as dull and boring, given that ninety percent of learning the language is memorizing characters. That is because many ABCs learned Chinese through Sunday Chinese school, which, although it proved to be useful, make the process even more monotonous than it seems by using aspects such as weekly memorization tests. Plus, many of us had to experience this for around nine to ten years, which proved too much for many people around me. Every year that I went back to the school, someone I knew would leave, and by the end of it, there were only around twenty kids left from the one hundred when I started.

Wow, so how bad is this process really? And if it was so bad, why did I continue? How did I manage to overcome these challenges?

Well, I guess you'll find out soon.

First of all, why did I even want to learn Chinese? The answer was because my grandparents spoke little to no English, and although my parents had learned English, they preferred to speak Chinese at home. We constantly met family friends who spoke Chinese rather than English. So, to be able to communicate effectively, I had to learn Chinese, which, although it was an easier learning process when compared to a language like Spanish, was still a whole other foreign language journey. Growing up in America with a family that spoke another language as their first language meant that instead of only having to learn one language when I was young, I basically had to learn two.

Learning the basics of English, like I said before, was relatively easy for me. This was because in preschool, everyone around me spoke English, I did my homework in English, and almost all my friends were American. Thus, I could practice English with them, which in turn led to my mastery of the basics of English faster. However, with Chinese, I didn't have many people to practice with besides my family. All my schoolwork and other English language things in my life, including drawing lessons, birthday parties, and sports, took up way too much of my time—too much for me to actually learn Chinese well. So, although I grew up in a bilingual family who spoke fifty percent English and fifty percent Chinese, my English was far more developed. Though I didn't think of myself as bad at Chinese, I never needed to speak it much, and the little I knew was usually enough.

Only when my family went to China for the first time, to visit family and friends, would I truly see how far behind my Chinese lagged, at least in comparison to my English.

I remember when I was in Shanghai one day. I was six and in kindergarten then, sitting in our hotel room, excited because my parents said that we would be going to a Chinese restaurant to meet my grandparents, who didn't live with us in America. I was very curious, and a little nervous. On the car ride there, I asked so many questions. What did my grandparents look like? How many people would be at the dinner? Would I get presents? Eventually, my parents got sick of it and told me to be quiet. But one thought kept lingering in my head: Would I be able to talk with them? I knew my Chinese wasn't the best, and I hoped that that wouldn't be the reason I wouldn't have a good time.

Turned out, sometimes, the thing you feared the most was exactly what happened.

When we got to the restaurant and entered the private dining room, I was immediately greeted not only by my grandparents but by my cousins, their friends, their grandparents, and even other people. It was a typical Chinese gathering. Around me, amidst the bright ceiling lights and the waiters bringing food, I heard many things, but no words were familiar to me besides the most basic ones: 你好 (ni hao → hello), 谢谢 (xie xie → thank you), and 红包 (hong bao → red envelope, used for a cash gift). When my grandparents came over and started talking to me, I failed to recognize even one full sentence. When they gave me a gift, even though I wanted to respond more politely, all I could say in Chinese was a simple thank you. That night, on the car ride back, I kept thinking about how I couldn't communicate at all. I kept telling myself that I should have done more to express my gratitude or enthusiasm about meeting them. It left a feeling of deep regret.

After that trip, although I had an excellent first impression of China, and I enjoyed many aspects of it—like the landmarks, the food, and the culture—the trip had also left me with a feeling, a feeling that

I was so weak in Chinese. My not so proficient Chinese skills had been exposed, and the fact that I couldn't understand anything prevented me from truly enjoying myself. Because of that, I started to despise the idea of ever returning to China. I knew that going back to China meant the same events happening again. So, I asked my mom: Are we ever going back to China again?

"Yes, many times. Why? You didn't like it?"

The truth was, I liked China—quite a lot. But the constraint that I couldn't speak Chinese made understanding the Chinese culture that I had started to love and appreciate much more difficult, so I was annoyed. But then, it was about me. What if I just got better at Chinese?

So, when I moved from New Jersey to Scarsdale during kindergarten, I saw that, nearby, there was a Chinese club. To prevent what happened in China from happening again, I enrolled in Sunday Chinese school. And though I didn't realize it at first, the Huaxia Chinese School was what was missing from my life. Its lack prevented my Chinese from improving.

When I walked through the doors of White Plains High School on day one of Chinese school, I didn't know what to expect. I hadn't taken a proper foreign language class before, so I was understandably worried, and a bit confused—even though I was taking a language that I had familiarity with. Many questions raced through my head as I walked to my classroom with my mom. Would the classes be hard? Would they even be interesting? Would I even understand anything at all? If I couldn't understand much in China, would it be the same here?

As the class started, the teacher began to tell us about the basics of Chinese, starting with Pinyin, the Chinese alphabet. I learned that there were twenty-three consonants and twenty-four vowels, and unfortunately I had to memorize them all. The teacher also taught us about the four tones in Chinese, ultimately teaching us that a

combination of these consonants, vowels, and tones made up Chinese words. Immediately, I could tell that these lessons were exactly what I needed to help improve my Chinese skills. But, by week three, I had become bored. Every class, it was just vocabulary and grammar, the same old rules and memorization exercises every single time. And the worst part? 听写 (ting xie → vocabulary testing). Each week before class we would memorize how to write each character, some of them really complex, and during class we would take a test to see how many we had memorized. Did I mention that these classes started early, so I had to wake up early? Every Saturday night, the day before Chinese school, I would walk up to my mom and say: "I don't want to go to Chinese school anymore, it's so boring and challenging."

My mom would calmly reply: "Well, you were the one who told me you wanted to sign up, and I already paid, so you better continue because I don't want to waste my money."

So, every Sunday morning, I had to drag myself to Chinese class. But one Sunday, it was as if the Chinese school teachers heard me complaining, because my Chinese teacher said: "Today, we're going to do something different." I immediately turned my head toward the

board, because that wasn't how these classes usually started. Normally, it was a test or a vocabulary review. Instead, my teacher told us to open our textbook, and flip to a page with a cartoon story. Instead of talking about new grammar rules and vocabulary, we started to read the story (The Tortoise and the Hare, to be exact but in Chinese). As we started reading, I began to feel more interested—a feeling that I never had before in Chinese school. I even volunteered to read a part of the story out loud, something I rarely ever did. As the class progressed line by line, I was intrigued by the information presented to me, and without the teacher's permission I read silently until the end of the story, before my class had finished.

Now, the habit of skipping ahead was something that I did not only then but still do now, as a teenager, I don't like to feel bored. As I started to realize that not only could Chinese school be beneficial in terms of language learning, but it could be quite fun—reading stories, learning about culture, and, occasionally, playing games, I continued to attend lessons every Sunday, complaining less and learning more. As the year progressed, I was able to master the Chinese alphabet. By spring, I learned many new Chinese characters, enough for me to have a decent conversation. And by summer, I finally learned how to read, write, and speak with modest fluency.

As the weeks turned into months, my journey through the first level of Chinese school became more rewarding than I could have ever imagined. Despite feeling confident in my understanding of the basics of Chinese at first, I learned that, similar to English, there was more to this language and culture than I thought. Every week I would learn something new or interesting that sparked my interest. This ranged from reading simple stories to learn new words to knowing more about China and it is culture. One of the most exciting moments for me was when I learned how to write my Chinese name. The intricate strokes and beautiful characters that form my name (毛逸清) conveyed a connection to my heritage, and a sense of identity. That was the moment that allowed me to feel connected to that part of who I was. Before taking Chinese lessons, I couldn't speak Chinese well, and I didn't know much about China or its culture. However, attending Chinese school allowed me to recognize the rich history and tradition within the Chinese language, and inspired me to delve even deeper into its intricacies.

Another moment that I vividly remember is when I first picked up a Chinese book. Not the ones that I was given in Chinese school but one given to me from my family. When I was small I loved to read, and nearly every day I would either read English-language books or ask my parents or grandparents to read me a story. However, up to this point, I was only capable of reading English books, as I had only learned English. When I learned enough Chinese from Chinese school to figure out bits and pieces of Chinese text, I thought that it might be interesting to start reading Chinese. So I chose the book that, at that time, seemed the most interesting: *Journey to the West*. Looking at the cover and the pictures, I saw a monkey wielding a stick, fighting monsters. I loved it. So, I picked up the book, opened to the first chapter, and was immediately sucked in. I read it non-stop for hours.

Even though I couldn't fully understand the story, I enjoyed my first Chinese book so much, and it inspired me to read other books to learn more. This not only further enhanced my Chinese skillsets but also allowed me to see extremely fascinating things within these stories. For example, through reading Journey to the West, I learned a lot about Chinese mythology, as the story revolves around Chinese gods.

By the end of my first year in Chinese school, I had learned most of the basic elements of Chinese, and with the advantage of having a Chinese family I mastered those elements pretty quickly. Along with the basics, I also learned many other new things, like idioms and their stories. My excitement and curiosity motivated me to continue attending Chinese school for many years. But before all that came a final exam of sorts, to see if all the hard work had paid off. I was going back to China again with my family, and I would try my best to make sure that what happened the year before wouldn't happen again.

There wasn't a major difference in our plan this time compared to the previous trip. We flew back to China mainly to visit families. We ate dinners together, met friends, and visited some new places, notably Beijing. Seemingly, nothing had changed. We did mostly the same things, yet I was having the time of my life, rather than feeling excluded. Why?

Because I had chosen to learn Chinese.

Unlike the last time, I could finally communicate. I no longer felt excluded, because of the language barrier. After learning some basic Chinese, I was able to truly connect, not just watching and listening but actually participating in conversations.

When I had dinner with my grandparents, I didn't just sit there, trying to decipher what they were saying. This time, I could clearly understand their basic requests, like "pass the soy sauce" or "try this dish." I could even have short conversations, asking about their day or sharing a funny story.

I could finally play with my cousins. We could play games, tell jokes, watch TV together, and laugh at the same funny scenes. We went to the arcade together and laughed at each other because we couldn't shoot a basketball. We went swimming and fought each other over who got the water gun. It was a whole new world of shared experiences, something that I didn't get to experience the last time I went to China. From the intricate calligraphy to the delicious food at the night market, I finally felt like I was at home within my secondary culture.

That was the moment when everything shifted. From then on, every year to my freshman year in high school, I would attend Chinese school every Sunday, partially because I wanted to learn more, and partially because I was forced to. Instead of playing video games or playing sports, I would wake up early and attend Chinese school, and this routine would last until two years ago. As months became years, I found myself progressing through the levels of Chinese school, climbing the ladder to mastery step by step. Each lesson brought new challenges, new discoveries, and a deeper understanding of the language. I immersed myself in captivating stories, wrote sentences, paragraphs, and essays, and explored aspects of Chinese culture with eager fascination. Learning both the language and the culture at Chinese school made the experience especially rewarding.

I also started exploring other aspects of the Chinese language. I thought that, by exposing myself to even more, my Chinese proficiency, and thus the quality of my experience in China, would improve. I would step onto the stage of the public speaking contest every year. I remember the first speech I gave, about the Chinese zodiac, where, even though I didn't win, I realized that I had potential. As long as I kept learning more advanced topics and kept practicing Chinese consistently with the people around me, I could achieve my goal of mastering the language. From then on, I gave a well-practiced speech every year at the speaking contest, ranging from well-known folk tales to stories that teach a serious lesson. The effort that I put into this competition was definitely worth it, as not only did I win a myriad of awards over the years (and a sore throat every November), I also gained more confidence in speaking Chinese. This immensely improved my knowledge of the language and put me a step closer to mastery.

I also participated in Chinese debates tournaments, practicing my ability to articulate my ideas in Chinese. It was a struggle at first, as I had never done anything like it in Chinese, yet, as I learned, through hard work anything is possible. So. I started writing and practicing with my mom and my teammates. I remember that every week or two we would all come together for debate practice. And even though I was the youngest, I still felt that I could keep up and was respected by my peers. At that moment, I knew that I could master the language. I could actually achieve the goal that I set for myself. Even though we only had minor success in my first year on the team, at this time in my life I began to truly enjoy Chinese. So, I rejoined the team for year two, ultimately ending up winning the tournament and best debater award. This, to me, was another test of mastery. I passed.

A year after the end of Chinese school, I found myself on a plane flying back to China during the winter break. Since Covid, I hadn't been back, so I was really excited to meet friends and family that I hadn't seen in a long time. I could finally utilize all those years of learning Chinese, because I wasn't going to China as a stubborn six-year-old; I was now a freshman and a successful Chinese school graduate. After returning to China, I found that what I had learned

in Chinese school allowed me to freely communicate with the people there, read Chinese labels, and much more. These new "tools" that I acquired allowed me to see China from a whole new perspective, and that made all those grueling Sundays spent sitting in a classroom worth it. Compared to the first time I was in China, where I could barely stutter simple words, now I was able to communicate with the natives, order my own food, and live a normal life.

My dedication to mastering Chinese led me to excel in the Advanced Placement (AP) Chinese exam. Utilizing the foundation laid at Chinese school and my experiences in China, I felt that preparing for this test was a piece of cake, and the test itself was, honestly, easier than my math test I took a day later. Because of the vast reservoir of knowledge I accumulated in Chinese school, the multiple choice, listening comprehension, and writing sections were quite easy.

My journey of studying the Chinese language has been transformative in ways beyond linguistic proficiency. It opened doors I haven't expected, and more importantly, allowed me to become immersed in Chinese culture itself.

And that made every one of those long Sunday mornings worth it.

Spanish

Una nueva lingua es una nueva vida.

— *Anonymous*

By the halfway point of my journey, I thought I had figured out how language learning worked. Spanish proved me wrong.

When I was young, I didn't even know that the Spanish language existed. For me, it was just English and Chinese—because those were the languages I grew up with. It wasn't until my family was planning a trip to Mexico in my second-grade year that I heard the word Spanish! One day, sitting at the table, eating my mac and cheese, my mom and dad came up to me. They started with the boring stuff, like "did you do your homework yet" and "you have a math class tonight." But then they said something completely unexpected.

"In November, we'll be going to Cancun."

"Where's that?"

"Mexico."

Going from talking about homework to visiting a new place? Now that was something that would make me jump up and down. If you couldn't tell by my initial reaction when I heard we were going to China—which was pretty similar to my reaction here—I really enjoy visiting new places. Why? Well, I was a little bored seeing the same house and neighborhood every day, and I've always been excited to see what a new place has in store for me. Plus, who doesn't love a break from school?

Because I was so excited about visiting Mexico, later I went on my mom's computer and searched the words "Cancun, Mexico." What I found were pictures of stunning white beaches with clear blue oceans, rich cultural heritage sites like the Mayan pyramids, and delicious food like tacos. These were things that I didn't get to see every day in America, making the trip even more exciting than when my parents brought it up. Just seeing the pictures made me wish for a superpower to fast-forward to the trip. However, after scrolling some more on the internet, I found something else that was quite interesting. Some of the names of the landmarks didn't sound familiar at all. Although they were still made up of the traditional alphabet, there were also accents over some of the vowels, Ns with a squiggly line on top, and word composition that broke the simple rules that I was taught. It was almost English—but with new flair. After thinking about it a little, I said to myself, "maybe this is a new language."

It turned out that it actually was.

After doing some more research, and confirming my suspicions with my family, I learned that, instead of English, Mexicans speak Spanish as their primary language—and at that point I knew absolutely zero Spanish. Thus, even though my mind was ninety percent filled with images of swimming in the ocean, looking at pyramids, and eating tacos, there was that ten percent that drifted elsewhere, since I probably couldn't communicate in Spanish. My mind briefly flashed back to that trip to China. I remembered that amidst all the fresh food, landmarks, and good memories, one thing bothered me: not being able to talk with them. I remembered how I felt on that car ride back, thinking that I should have done more to talk to them, to express my gratitude, but I just couldn't. At that point, however, I didn't think too much about it. I was a child, and when you expose a child to something interesting, it doesn't stick in their head for too long.

As the next school year approached, I thought it would be another normal school year, where I would continue building upon my knowledge in science class, English class, math class... However, when I walked in on the first day, my teacher made an announcement that would change everything.

"This year, we will be introducing something new: foreign language classes."

I was shocked. This opportunity couldn't have come at a better time. My hand shot up, and I asked: "What languages?" My teacher replied: "Spanish and French."

Ever since the day when I learned that I would be going to Cancun, thoughts of learning Spanish occasionally popped up. Given my knowledge of learning English and Chinese, I understood that searching for simple words online wasn't going to cut it. Learning a language takes time, consistency, and constant practice, and quite honestly I couldn't find time or any suitable opportunities—so I had let the idea drop. But when I heard this, I immediately knew that I had to take Spanish. This opportunity—that came out of nowhere—felt like the best thing that could have happened to me. My constant dreaming about Mexico pushed me to sign up for Spanish. Who knew, maybe I'd even learn something about Cancun?

As my first Spanish class approached, I felt a mixture of excitement and nervousness swirling inside of me, just like my first day of Chinese school. Many thoughts raced through my mind, most of them which were the same as my first day of learning any other language.What if I couldn't keep up? Would the class be different from other classes?

Despite these anxieties, I was still interested in Spanish, and the class would be fun. Another thing I told myself was that I wouldn't be starting from zero. I had already experienced the process of learning a new language twice, and kind of succeeded. So why wouldn't the third time be the same? The third time's the charm, right? Armed with this newfound motivation, I stepped into the classroom on the first day, eager to embark on this new journey.

I was immediately greeted by the enthusiasm and the welcoming presence of my teacher. With a warm smile, he introduced himself and told us to sit on the colorful rug in front of the computer. As I looked around the classroom, I was amazed by the bright colors and unique objects around the classroom. For example, I noticed the different flags hanging from the ceiling, surrounding us in a blend of red, blue, yellow, green, and many other colors. I saw the five yellow stars on a red field that I was familiar with, and I saw the stars and stripes that represented my birthplace. Yet I also saw new flags, where the sun rose through blue-and-white stripes, a green flag with a globe in its center, encompassed by a yellow diamond, and an eagle flying through red, white, and green.

Eventually, I settled in. Once the class began, I knew it was different. The way the teacher taught, his passion for the language, and the way he expressed his genuine excitement for sharing the culture of the Spanish language all truly motivated me. He asked all of us: "Why did you sign up for Spanish?" I replied: "Because my family is going to Cancun later this year." Amidst all the jealous looks from the classmates, my teacher, with a smile, said: "Wow, I hope you enjoy Mexico! Even better, you can try out what we'll have learned in this class!" Just hearing that made me realize that this class was going to be good. I was not only going to learn something new: it was going to help me have a better time in Cancun.

Our teacher did everything to make the class fun and enjoyable. For example, for our first exercise, we played Quizlet Live to review the materials we learned. Although that might seem quite boring now that I am in high school, for a second grader I was very intrigued by the matching game. And not only did it help me learn Spanish, it also gave me an opportunity to show off to my friends (I got first place). Stepping out of the classroom that day, I felt that my decision to enroll in Spanish was definitely the right decision. Not only did it help with my personal goal of being able to communicate when I went to Mexico, it also served as an interesting and low-stakes class that gave me a break during the day. This was the best first foreign language class experience that I could have had. Whether it was that I hadn't known any Spanish, or that my Spanish teacher made an effort to make the class into a fun one, my first day of Spanish started off with a bang.

As the first weeks of my Spanish learning journey went by, I could tell how much I loved the class. Every day, my teacher would bring that same energy to class, and he tried his best to make every single class both informational and interesting. It's like he drank a five-hour energy drink before each class, because every single class would be so vibrant and enthusiastic. Thanks to his teaching methods, the Spanish alphabet would forever stick in my head—thanks to a song that my class thought was hilarious. I learned the lyrics just so I could beat my friends at Quizlet, and the "Maestro puedo ir al baño (Teacher, may I go to the bathroom)?" song was one of the funniest things to me as a child.

As weeks turned into months, Spanish class never ceased to interest and amaze. Learning about the language itself, as well as the beautiful culture of not just Spain but Spanish-speaking countries as well, was enlightening. Every day, I would walk into that colorful and vibrant classroom ready to learn Spanish, win games, and have a lot of fun. One moment that I remember especially well was the first time I became capable of introducing myself in Spanish. Even though it wasn't perfect, as I stuttered here and there, and watched others laugh at me as I struggled to roll my rs (which I still do), for me it was a huge accomplishment. Being able to confidently tell others who I was gave me a sense of pride—along with a sense of belonging, a feeling that I was part of Spanish culture. Yet this moment was just one of many special moments along my Spanish journey that year. I learned how to describe the weather, my favorite foods, and much more. By the end of the year, even though I hadn't mastered or even utilized much of the language, I learned the basics. That was a good first step.

Then came the trip. A day after getting out of my final Spanish class before Thanksgiving break, I found myself on a plane to Cancun, arguing with my grandma about sleeping on such a short flight. As we began our descent into Mexico, I woke up to the normal English crew announcements, the normal "prepare for descent" and "fasten your seatbelt" calls. However, as I tried to finish my movie, another broadcast was made. This time, it was in what I presumed to be Spanish. Different from a classroom setting, the announcers spoke at such a fast pace and used such complex words that it basically sounded like gibberish—aside from the first word, "hola," and the last word, "gracias." My parents jokingly said: "Felix, you learned Spanish, what are they saying?"

All I could say was "I have no idea."

Stepping out of the plane into the hot Mexico sun, everything slowed down and felt more comprehensible. Then, when my family went to get food, I would find out in an embarrassing way how wrong I was.

After our flight, we were understandably hungry. We went to get the most Mexican food that we could think of: tacos. We arrived at the restaurant, and immediately I was tasked with ordering our food. I was stumped. Although we learned some basic phrases in class, we never learned certain vocabulary. Additionally, being in a real world situation, with a waiter staring over you, added a ton of pressure.

Amidst all the confusion, I was finally able to mumble out the words, and what should have been a fluent conversation ended up being a combination of me saying "dos ... these things ... por favor" while pointing to the menu awkwardly, and my mom added, "Give him some time, he just started learning Spanish."

The waiter seemed to understand my effort, however, and said "gracias" with a smile—but no smile or comfort could relieve the awkwardness.

As I was waiting for the tacos to come, I stared at the menu, and the words "carne asada," "elote," "chicharrones" flew through my head. They seemed so familiar, yet so unfamiliar at the same time. Was this really the Spanish I learned?

"Know anything the menu says?" My mom asked me.

"Uhhh... no."

Amid the laughter from my family and the sarcastic "I thought you knew Spanish" comments from my sister, I felt ... terrible.

When the tacos came, I just stared at them, as if I was praying at the taco gods to make me magically know Spanish. The thought that I couldn't even have a conversation after spending so much time learning Spanish troubled me.

As soon as I took a bite of what was probably the best taco I've ever eaten, I forgot about this.

As the trip went on, similar moments kept happening, and things started to feel a lot like that trip to China. Good food, good views, good everything, but awkward moments. But how could that be? I had planned, studied, but I still couldn't hold a simple conversation. I didn't want to feel that way anymore.

Well, I wouldn't realize this until I grew older, but as interesting as I did find my first two months of Spanish, most of my Spanish practice had been in a classroom, with a bunch of other kids who were trying to learn. Compared to Chinese and English, where I was able to practice with fluent speakers all the time, my Spanish practice sessions were different.

That brings up another aspect of learning languages. Learning in a classroom can be very different from learning in the real world—and I wasn't ready for it.

That's why, when learning a language, you should try and make it immersive and simulate real-life situations. You can learn as much about the language as you can in a classroom and then go out there and not be able to do anything (as my example showed). However, that doesn't mean that what you learn in a classroom doesn't help you; it's just that with simulated real-life conversations the practice and effort you put in will be much more effective. But back to my story.

At the end of second grade, my introduction to Spanish came to a close, and to say that I was very intrigued about this fascinating foreign language was a complete understatement. Due to my teacher's enthusiastic teaching methods, as well as his efforts to make every single class interesting, I found myself extremely eager to continue this journey of learning Spanish. So, when third grade came around, I signed up for Spanish class without any hesitation.

I would feel the same way about Spanish class up to the fifth grade, my last year of elementary school. Each day, I would eagerly anticipate stepping into that vibrant classroom that we all knew and loved, that same classroom that stunned me the first time I stepped into it. The constant laughter and joy made learning Spanish a very fun thing to do. Activities like playing Spanish games and watching Spanish movies also made the lessons feel more like entertainment than like work. Before I knew it, I had already learned so much about the Spanish language that I could recite vocabulary and phrases with ease, talk about daily aspects of my life, and much more. As my skills progressed, so did my self-assurance. I began to take pride in my Spanish speaking abilities. Each time I spoke Spanish, I felt a rush of excitement and accomplishment, as if I was bridging a gap between cultures.

However, during the middle of my fifth grade year I realized that this would be the last year I took Spanish with my elementary school teacher, because I would be transitioning to a new school. I had so many great memories of my Spanish teacher. He had the remarkable ability to make each lesson engaging and meaningful and was my and my classmates' favorite teacher. We shared so much laughter, explored so many fascinating cultural topics, and tackled the challenges of learning Spanish together in an engaging and fun way. Thus, I was understandably sad that I would be concluding my elementary school Spanish journey, knowing that I would soon be saying goodbye to not just a teacher but also a mentor who had nurtured my love for the language.

Yet, amidst these bittersweet feelings, I was also excited about my new school, and I would continue taking Spanish there. The idea of meeting new classmates and a new teacher who shared the same enthusiasm I had for them was exciting, and I imagined us engaging in lively discussions, participating in fun and immersive activities, and taking on new challenges to further improve my language skills. It's safe to say that I had pretty high expectations.

Then Covid struck.

I had picked probably the worst year to transition to a new school, as online classes, quarantine, and much more became the norm. Things became more isolated and more boring because of the masks and online classes, especially in Spanish. When I walked into my new sixth grade Spanish class on the first day of school, it wasn't the colorful and energetic classroom that I was used to. Instead of the flags of countries around the world were charts of what I assumed were grammar rules, and instead of the rug we always sat on in class were three rows of normal classroom chairs. The masks, plexiglass dividers, and the giant TV in the corner with Mashme (similar to Zoom but exponentially worse) set up on it made the setting far more mundane than it actually was. I wasn't sure if it was the teacher's fault or the Covid restrictions—maybe a combination of both—that made these classes less interactive, and which completely removed the immersive part of Spanish class. And as I mentioned above, that was what allowed my Spanish to improve and what allowed me to have fun in class. Instead of the interactive exercises, the funny videos, and the competitive games, it was just reading from a textbook for what felt like ninety percent of the class. The energetic "hola, cómo estás?" was gone, replaced by "dame su tarea!" (Turn in your homework!).

These factors made my sixth grade Spanish experience on the whole quite boring, and far worse than what I had anticipated. Even though I was still learning new and more complex information, such as verb conjugations and new vocabulary, the enthusiasm and color of my elementary school class was missing. After that year, I began to question myself. Did my elementary school Spanish classes actually represent what Spanish class was normally like? I had so much fun at my previous school, but when I transitioned to my new school, Spanish class became excruciating.

So, I hesitated to take Spanish the next year. I asked myself, if Spanish was going to be so boring—and also quite hard—why bother? Maybe it was time to take another language, like Latin, or French.

But my gut feeling told me to continue. I had already discovered and experienced so many interesting things about Spanish—maybe more was in store for me? So, I hesitantly signed up for Spanish.

However, with Covid restrictions beginning to ease, classrooms started to open up and become more interactive. I realized that the previous year was just a one-time thing, caused by special circumstances. The immersive, vibrant, and interesting Spanish class I had become accustomed to in elementary school was back. Teachers, again with more freedom, began incorporating more interactive activities—things we weren't allowed to do during Covid, like group discussions and hands-on projects. This was especially evident in our Spanish class, with interactive games and activities. For example, we started to play many of the games that I used to play in elementary school, such as Kahoot and Quizlet, to increase interactivity and to make class more fun. We were able to do group projects, which also increased the overall experience of the class. Spanish class in my new school shifted from a solitary struggle with verb conjugations and vocabulary to lively conversations and engaging exercises that actually simulated real-life situations. After seventh grade, it seemed that last year's Spanish class was just an exception due to Covid. Spanish classes would still be as interactive and exciting as what I knew and loved.

That year, up until the end of middle school, I worked on the basics of Spanish grammar, drastically increased my Spanish vocabulary, and, most importantly, learned a lot about Spanish-language culture. We learned songs to sing along with. We performed skits, some so funny that it was hard to pay serious attention. And to make it even better, I was having fun playing games, singing, acting, and learning. That was what I expected advanced Spanish class to be like.

Finally, after three years of ups and downs and everything in-between (which, believe it or not, was just the start), I was ready to take the next step on my Spanish journey: high school Spanish. Entering ninth grade, I had my worries and doubts, similar to when I transitioned from elementary to middle school. Most of my worries were about the class being too difficult or me not being able to keep up. But like my previous experiences, a single class would show me that I didn't need to worry at all, at least for the time being.

When I walked into the classroom, I couldn't help but notice how similar it was to my elementary school. Again vivid, again full of flags (different ones this time), and also paintings. Most importantly, my ninth-grade Spanish teacher resembled my elementary school teacher more than any of my other teachers. Walking in, we were energetically greeted in Spanish, with "Hola clase!" and "Que ta pasando (what's up)?" He had a sense of ease and energy that I hadn't seen in a long time, and after seeing that some of the first activities we would do were games and other interactive exercises, I immediately knew that this Spanish class would be like no other.

It was in that vibrant setting that I had the opportunity to dive into not only advanced grammar, literature, and real-world applications of the language but also culture, the reading of Spanish books, singing songs, and learning about Spanish-speaking communities around the world. It propelled my language skills further than ever before, thanks to my teacher and my classmates. However, it wasn't a simple walk in the park. That year was actually the hardest and most intense I had. Not only was the grammar and vocabulary getting much more complicated, with our class learning new past, future, and conditional tenses, but my Spanish teacher also introduced a new element: oral exams. In these exams he would interview us about a book we read, oftentimes material I hadn't even fully understood, and we had to respond in (hopefully) fluent Spanish. Additionally, the fast-paced Spanish that he spoke with often left me and my friends dumbfounded. Previously, our teachers would use a combination of Spanish and English, so it was hard transitioning to a Spanish-only class. Thus, my understanding of the new and quite difficult material wasn't that great. The upcoming first oral exam didn't help the situation at all.

On the morning of the oral exam, I walked into the classroom prepared—or so I thought. Even though I was mentally prepared and had spent the last night studying with my classmates, that morning my voice seemed to… vanish. When my turn came, I nervously walked out to the teacher, who had a timer and a notepad waiting on the table. "Esta listo? (Are you ready?)"

"I guess…"

Famous last words…

As he asked the first question, my head started to spin. No concrete thoughts came to me. I began to stutter: "Yo… pienso que… (I… think that…)," and when half the time had passed I finally finished my answer. I looked up at my teacher, jotting notes in his book. One eyebrow was raised, and he had a look of confusion.

Not good.

After another two questions, the nightmare finally ended. When it came to feedback, I was, simply put, embarrassed. I wasn't able to use the simple conjugations that he taught me, my vocabulary was poor, and I, quite frankly, felt stupid. But the last thing that my Spanish teacher said at least made me feel a little better.

"Felix, I know you have the capability to do better, you just have to practice."

After that test, I went home and tried to continue my day—but the exam wouldn't leave me. I had failed. But the worst part was that, apparently, I could have excelled. There was no part of me that was thinking about excelling, however; it was only struggle and not being able to learn the language. Were the other two languages a fluke? Was it because my family is bilingual that I could learn English and Chinese so easily but not Spanish?

And that's when it hit me. I had been in these situations before. These same exact situations. The moments when I was struggling with learning and not understanding the material. I thought back to when I was struggling to learn English. I remembered how I was in the same situation three years earlier, a kid in a new setting trying to learn something and struggling at it. I couldn't help but notice the parallels to the situation I was in. However, I also remembered how I got out of that hole: asking for help. After thinking about it, I told myself: If it worked once, why won't it work twice?

So, despite looks of embarrassment from those around me, I talked with my Spanish teacher, and we set up weekly meetings to talk freely in Spanish. Sports, holidays, my life—we could talk about whatever we wanted. I even told him about an upcoming trip to Costa Rica—we planned it because my sister started to love birds—and he responded very similarly to the way my elementary school teacher responded when I told him about my trip to Cancun. As time went on, the conversations became more natural. This is just one example of how you can practice as much as you want in a classroom and it still won't match the experience of immersion.

One day, I walked into my Spanish teacher's room during office hours, expecting a normal prep lesson, and I saw he was holding a set of strange dice in his hand. Instead of dots, these dice had pictures—a fish, a house, a sun. Before I could even put my backpack down, he smiled and slid them across toward me.

"Roll them."

I picked them up, shook them in my cupped hands the way you would at a board game table, and tossed them onto the desk. They clattered and spun and settled. I looked down: a fish. A house. A clock. A pair of shoes.

"Now," he said, leaning back in his chair with that familiar look that meant he already knew this was going to be interesting, "tell me a story. In Spanish. Using all of them."

I paused. What? How would I be able to do this? A few months ago, that pause would have stretched into complete blankness, the kind where your mind went completely blank and the only Spanish word you could remember is hola.

Yet this time, something clicked. I started talking. Slowly at first, I messed up conjugations and vocabulary here and there, but eventually, I told a ridiculous story. It was about a man who lived in a house by the sea and lost his shoes chasing a fish.

My teacher didn't interrupt. He just listened, nodding occasionally, and when I finally finished, he laughed.

"See?" he said. "Your Spanish is so much better than you think."

And he was right. For those two or three minutes, I had just been speaking some of the best Spanish of my life. It wasn't perfect—but for the first time, it felt natural, and became instinctual. I wasn't translating any more. I was just speaking. And for the first time in a long while, I started to enjoy Spanish again.

That was when things started to change.

These lessons went on for around two months, and by the time the next oral exam came around, I treated it not with fear but with confidence. I already knew I could maintain a conversation with my teacher. And sure enough, the first thing he said after that exam was: "Felix, I knew you could do it." To test my Spanish skills in real life, which I now understood was important to mastering a language, I went to Costa Rica and challenged myself to speak Spanish with the locals. Although I still felt awkward at times, as I struggled to find the right word, I was still capable of engaging in short conversations and could be a not-so-helpful translator when my parents needed it—thanks to the practice and work I put in.

However, not only were our one-on-one conversations beneficial for my studies, they also allowed me to get to know my Spanish teacher better as a person. He would go on to teach me for two years (9th and 10th grades), and every single day he made Spanish class something I could look forward to. So, when I found out that he was leaving after that year, and I wouldn't be able to take AP Spanish the next year, I felt that my Spanish journey, at least for the time being, was coming to a close. But there was something I still wanted to do. I wanted to end this chapter of my Spanish journey on a high note, and there was the perfect opportunity.

In my sophomore year, our school hosted a student exchange program for all three modern languages, and the Spanish trip was in

Barcelona. I saw it as a wonderful opportunity as well as a vacation—especially because it was right after the school year ended (and I was also a huge FC Barcelona fan). However, I knew that the main reason these programs were created was to give students an immersive experience, and I was also up for that challenge. So, I filled out the form, and to my surprise was selected to be a part of the program.

My first memory of my exchange partner was when our Spanish counterparts came to our school around March and lived with us. I was looking forward to getting to know my counterpart, and I was able to do that. Whether it was through our common love of FC Barcelona, playing soccer together, or getting him addicted to American fast food, the experience allowed me to build a connection. When we took him around New York, it felt like nothing special to me—I was too used to it, all of the landmarks and the culture. However, I know that, for my counterpart, it was definitely a culture shock. It was one of the most unique trips of his life.

Three months later, our roles were reversed, and it was I who was going through that culture shock, marveling at all the wonderful things about life in Barcelona. On my first day there, I was met by a welcoming and warm environment. My host family, the people at the school, everyone was so warm and friendly. Although they mostly spoke in Spanish, and their English wasn't the best, thanks to what I learned in Spanish class over the years I could have simple conversations, and could understand that I was most certainly welcome there—and would definitely have a great time.

My first shock came during lunch, where I soon found out that Spanish people ate lunch at three and dinner at nine. When I asked, my counterpart merely said "because Spanish people are kind of laid back, it's kind of the culture here." So even though I was constantly starving, I felt happy, because I was experiencing what it was truly like to be Spanish.

I also found communicating, the single aspect that I worried about the most, to be quite easy. I don't know if it was the conversations with my teacher that helped, or that I had studied Spanish for such a long time, but I was able to converse quite fluently, including ordering food, greeting people, and showing gratitude. Every day, I felt quite comfortable using a little Spanish. For example, in the morning, my friends and I would always go to this snack stand outside the school, and without pressure, I would say "puedo comprar ...?" (can I buy _?). So much so that even the vendor was surprised, given the fact that she knew I wasn't native.

It was this capability—to somewhat understand what was going on—that made the landmarks I went to more breathtaking, the food I tasted more delicious, and the daily life I experienced more authentic. For example, when we visited La Sagrada Familia, I was looking at the Spanish words engraved into metal signs that gave an overview of what the church was. This reminded me of something: my trip to Cancun in first grade. Back then, I remembered how at the Mayan Pyramids, I saw similar metal signs with Spanish on them, yet then, those words were still gibberish. Now, I didn't know all the words there, but I was still able to recognize and understand certain aspects of that metal sign, such as how the interior of the church was heavily inspired by nature and that it was built in 1882. Now, being able to read this sign, I started to feel a sense of pride, a feeling that all the progress I made along this seven-year journey was worth it.

This trip was probably the most immersed I had been in another culture, because I was actually living the life of a teenager in Spain.

I remember that one night, where my friends and I, along with our counterparts, went into the city to dinner. As I walked along the streets of Barcelona with friends, both old and new, Spanish and American, I began to feel the influence of language. As we sat down at a pasta restaurant, I picked up a menu written in Spanish. Yet this time, I was able to order for myself, something I couldn't do in Mexico. As we waited for the food, the conversations started to flow.

"What was school in America like?" "Who's the best soccer player out of you guys?" "Who's your favorite musician?"

The conversation kept slipping between English and Spanish almost without anyone noticing, one of my American friends cracking a joke in English that my Spanish friend somehow caught anyway. By the time the food arrived, it no longer felt like a cultural exchange, just dinner with friends. Even though it seemed like quite a normal activity, the laughter and warmth the ten of us created was something that I'll remember forever, because it was something that made me feel like I lived in Spain and was just like one of them. Whether it was complaining to my counterpart about how far we had to walk, or the days I spent following my counterpart around doing what he usually

did, I was able to, more than any other trip in my life, experience and immerse myself in a culture in a different part of the world. Ultimately, through this trip, I was able to not only visit the landmarks in Barcelona, especially places that interested me like Camp Nou and Sitges, but also understand how people in Barcelona live their lives. It was the perfect way to end that chapter of my Spanish Journey.

All in all, I don't have a single regret about learning Spanish. A simple trip to Mexico showed me a new realm, and the journey in that new realm was, is, and will be one that I will never forget. I'm positive that the future will have more for me, even if I won't be taking Spanish class next year.

Latin

Nova lingua est vita nova.

— *Anonymous*

At this point in the book, you're probably asking yourself how many languages is this guy going to learn? That was my thought as well, when Latin was first presented to me. At that point in my life, language-wise, I was in eighth grade, I had commanded English, had just graduated Chinese school, and was improving quite a bit at Spanish. However, when I was discussing course selections with my teachers and family, the idea of taking Latin popped up.

Latin seemed like just another boring language, and there were reasons no one spoke it anymore. I also had friends who took Latin, and from what I had briefly heard and seen, I wasn't impressed. That was why—when I was originally faced with the decision between taking Spanish, French, or Latin in school—I chose Spanish. So, when my mom asked me to consider Latin, my first reaction was a hard "no." I reasoned that Latin would just be another class in my already-packed schedule, meaning that I would also have to spend a massive amount of time learning yet another language—one that, apparently, was the most complex one.

Nevertheless, there was still a part of me that wanted to try it. I had always been interested in classical culture, especially the mythology. During elementary school, I read the Percy Jackson series after a friend recommended it and was immediately drawn into the world of gods and their stories. I found all the supernatural abilities and the stories about gods, demigods, and heroes utterly fascinating. From Percy's fight with the Minotaur to the Sea of Monsters and the battle against Cronos, I was captivated. There were the arcs of lightning shooting from Zeus' bolt, the love stories, the betrayals, and the friendship—all of it drew me in. It was those stories that really interested me as part of Latin culture, and I decided to choose Greek mythology as my capstone project in fifth grade.

However, I was still not sure about taking Latin, and my interest in Percy Jackson wasn't enough to convince me. But, as if some supernatural force wanted me to take Latin, on a whim I chatted with one of my friends, and I brought up that I was thinking about Latin next year.

Surprisingly, he said: "Me too!"

After that we talked a little, and he introduced me to the huge academic upside that Latin could offer. For example, it would help in subjects like English and Spanish, because many words from both languages come from Latin, as well as some of the grammar. I was surprised by the upside of taking Latin. And, to address the rumor of Latin being hard, I felt that if my friend was there to support me, I would be fine. In the worst case, we would struggle for one month and drop the class together.

I walked in on the first day alongside my friend and one other student who soon became a good friend. The three of us filed in and looked around. It was immediately clear that I was not in Spanish class anymore. My Spanish classrooms had felt almost alive: bright flags, colorful rugs, the constant low hum of someone conjugating

something under their breath. Not this room. This room had a different energy entirely. There were posters, sure, but they looked like they had been on those walls for decades, depicting marble busts of philosophers who looked like they had never smiled once in their entire lives.

I had always heard the phrase "dead language" and kind of nodded along without really knowing what it meant. Sitting in that classroom, looking at those posters, I finally got it.

It got more real when class actually started. Unlike every other language class I had ever taken, this one was taught entirely in English. There was no "Hola clase," no warm greeting in the target language, no attempt to drop you into the deep end and see if you could swim. Just English. A simple line of "welcome to Latin" by my teacher who I could tell was trying to revive this dead language.

Most of our classmates had been studying Latin since middle school and were already a level or two ahead, which meant the three of us were essentially playing catch-up. Our teacher made it very clear within the first ten minutes that to catch up, we would be covering

Latin 1 and Latin 2 simultaneously so that by the end of the year we could rejoin our grade level.

What?

I looked over at my friend. He looked back at me and mouthed: "What did we get ourselves into? How hard is this class?"

Well, the answer was: very. It would be very hard.

Luckily, we had a great teacher. Although she didn't sugarcoat that this class could be boring, or challenging at times, she always brought an enthusiastic and encouraging attitude. Walking out that day, my friend and I agreed that she was one of the nicest teachers we had. But we also agreed on something else.

"This class seems hard!"

And believe me, it would be hard—really hard. Even though that wasn't what it seemed like at first.

During the first week or so of classes, my friend and I felt better about the class. We were introduced to the basics of Latin, including nouns, verbs, and adjectives. Since I had some background in learning languages somewhat related to Latin, it was pretty easy for me to pick up. Although it came at a really fast pace, I enjoyed the thrill of learning my first new words, like "amo" and "amare" for love, and "puer" and "pueri" for boys. Even though they were simple words, they were the first steps in my Latin journey. My friend was equally enthusiastic and given that he also had a language learning background, we found ourselves working together in an attempt to master what we had just learned.

Soon came our first test.

The night before, my friend and I hunched over our phones on FaceTime for what felt like hours, drilling conjugations, declensions, and vocabulary. We quizzed each other, corrected each other, and by the time I went to bed, I felt ready.

Walking into the classroom the next morning, though, that confidence had a slight wobble. This was the first time any of what I had learned would actually be tested. But I kept reminding myself: I knew this material. I had gone over it a hundred times. I was fine.

As I completed the first section, that's exactly what I felt. Vocabulary, conjugations, declensions—everything was a piece of cake.

I started to relax. Then I started to feel good. Then, I'll be honest, I started thinking about how I was going to describe this test to my classmates afterward. "What an easy test!" "See, this class wasn't going to be so bad after all."

Then I turned the page to the sentence translation section, and every single one of those thoughts evaporated.

The sentences just sat there on the page, staring back at me. I knew every individual word. I knew the grammar rules. But the moment they were combined into an actual sentence, something in my brain just… stopped. What does this word mean in this context? Why is the verb at the end? What case is this—and why does it matter here?

The clock on the wall, which I had barely noticed during the first section, suddenly became the loudest thing in the room. I wrote things down. Crossed them out. Wrote them down again. When time was finally called, I looked at my paper and saw what was essentially a record of my own panic.

I walked out into the hallway and turned to my friends. The only thing I could think to say was: "What in the world was that?"

The look on their faces told me everything I needed to know. It wasn't just me.

That helped, at least a little. But it didn't answer the question that had already begun forming in the back of my head—the one that would bother me for the rest of the day: if I had studied every individual piece, why couldn't I put them together when it actually counted?

This goes back to the immersion and application aspects of language learning. Being a dead language, there isn't really a way to practice speaking it conversationally—but, in a sense, translating sentences and putting the grammar and vocabulary together imitates immersion. And as we learned from my experiences with Spanish, classroom practice isn't enough. Application is equally important as well when it comes to learning a language.

This would be a pattern for the rest of the year. We'd learn something new, that built on what we learned, with a difficult caveat for every unit. Then the test would come. Every other section would be easy, but the sentence translation section would be incredibly difficult—although, as I learned more and practiced more, it did get a little easier. Fortunately, our teacher, once again showing her supportive and kind side, allowed us to correct our tests—so we could still manage to get good scores, and continue to be motivated to learn Latin. Otherwise, who knows how bad my grades could have been. It might have even put that B that I got in 6th grade English to shame.

As the days passed, we delved deeper into the intricacies of noun cases and verb conjugations. The first few lessons were largely focused on the simple stuff, like the first two verb conjugations and declensions, and adjectives. Given the fast pace of the class, we were learning new things every time. However, it wasn't just grammar in every single class. Our teacher also took time to introduce us to Roman culture—teaching us about Ancient Rome, its myths, and more. The first story we read was about Icarus, the boy who flew too close to the sun. However, this was the first time I read the story in Latin, which made everything difficult and puzzling—but also more interesting at the same time, since it was from a Roman perspective. In parallel to our readings, our teacher shared more about Ancient Rome, such as its aqueducts and how they were designed.

As the first months came to a close, I felt extremely happy that I chose to learn Latin. For one, I had picked up yet another language pretty quickly, and I enjoyed many things about it, like its grammar and the history. I could also tell that learning Latin helped with my other subjects. For example, in English class, I felt that material related to vocabulary that I once thought to be difficult seemed easier, as learning Latin roots indirectly helped my English vocabulary. Also, in Spanish class, my vocabulary grew—thanks to the similarities between Spanish and Latin. During those conversations I had with my Spanish teacher, he would say: "Looks like someone's been practicing vocab!"

However, as I learned more, at the same time the information started to become more complicated, and I started to feel overwhelmed by the complexity. As new grammar rules piled up, as well as the rest of the conjugations and declensions, new adjective

rules, and, worst of all, participles (one of the hardest things I've ever learned, not just language-wise), the class got harder and harder, and I had to dedicate more time to understanding the material. I remember, one day, a random day in mid-January, I walked happily into class with my friend—but walked out like the world had just ended. That was the day we learned about participles, and I wasn't sure if I had experienced anything harder. My friend, who had class both before and after with me, asked me in the later class what happened. It was like I had put on a mask with a completely different identity.

From then on, the material didn't get any easier. It would continue to get harder and harder and harder up until our finals (which were in March). For nights before the final I stressed more over this specific exam than any other, and studied the conjugations, grammar rules, and most importantly sentence translations, over and over and over with my friends. As for the final, it was structured more or less the same as a normal test, with the sentence translation being the hardest part. The worst part? We didn't get to correct our tests, so we had to get everything perfect on the first try.

After our Latin final was over, I felt that, for one, I needed a break, and for two, I was a lot less motivated to continue taking Latin. The past few months made me understand it was way too hard of a class.

Countless nights I studied with my friends, memorizing declension tables and grammatical exceptions. And after every test we would group together in the library, puzzling over why every test was so damn hard (and also thanking God that we could do corrections). Since we were taking an intensive course, I had to learn double the material of a normal Latin class in the same amount of time. Thus, the schedule for our classes was often to learn, test, and then immediately learn something new. It was much faster than any other class. This caused me some burnout, and the thought of quitting Latin popped into my head.

However, amidst all the challenges, I also experienced moments of success that made the hard work seem worthwhile. I remember when I started to consistently translate sentences correctly, after weeks of struggling and getting things wrong. At the start of the year, when my classmates and I studied together, we felt lost. However, we all experienced a breakthrough in the language around the same time, suddenly beginning to understand everything. This sense of success was exactly what I needed to reignite my passion for Latin. It was a reminder that, if you put in the work, it will pay off. And I had put in the work. Just like with other languages before, I would face struggles and challenges, but as long as I continued, success would come.

With this new mindset toward improvement, I began to feel more comfortable with the language, allowing me to find the fun side of Latin. As we learned more, we unlocked new areas that we could explore—similar to other languages. The readings and activities opened up a new world of literature that was rich in history and culture. Though it isn't alive currently, it still had a huge impact on the world. Examples of Latin culture include the classics, such as poems by Cicero and Virgil, as well as myths about Hercules, Pandora's Box, and the twelve Olympian gods (the same ones I was intrigued by when I was a child). These activities not only reinforced my understanding of the vocabulary and grammar that we had learned but also introduced a fun and interesting side to the language and allowed me to appreciate the beauty of Latin.

After a year of arduous studying to catch up to my fellow ninth graders, I believed that taking Latin was definitely the right decision. Each and every Latin lesson felt like an adventure, sometimes easy, sometimes hard. Sometimes it was boring, but sometimes it was filled with wonder. It did have rocky moments, but with the help of our teacher, I was able to continue the journey. To her, our mistakes weren't setbacks, they were steppingstones that helped us improve—so much so that she allowed us to do corrections on tests, something that other teachers rarely did. She also had a plethora of other activities to make a four-person class feel better. More importantly, she helped us build a great foundation for the language, and most certainly set us up well for the following year, when we would be joining the rest of the kids in our grade. She was definitely a big part of why I was able to pick up this grammatically dense and complex language in only a year, compared to the five or six years my friends had been taking.

But this brought up some concerns. Next year, I would be taking a normal Latin class. I still questioned if I would be up to the skill level of students who had studied it for years. It wasn't just me—all the students in my class were thinking the same thing.

And when I began my tenth-grade Latin class, that was what I felt. From my first impression, I noticed that the people around me looked like naturals speaking the language, while mine was a bit clunky. I could also tell that this was the case for some of my friends too. Surprisingly, though, when it came to the actual information, I saw that I wasn't that far behind. Even though the actual learning process was rushed, we still had a decent foundation. Maybe it was because of the intensity with which I learned Latin last year, but I was actually doing better than some of the people who had been taking it since middle school. This made the class feel less tumultuous. Thanks to last year, I wasn't used to not learning new things in every single Latin class. I don't know if that was a good thing—the workload got easier—or a bad thing—the class seemed more boring. It wasn't the teacher's fault or anything like that, it was just the fact that I got used to a fast-paced class.

However, there were definitely times when the class was the exact opposite of boring. Besides the times when my friends and I made fools out of ourselves for guessing what a word meant, or laughing over a stupid mistake on a test, we learned more grammar, like conditions and clauses, and we were able to start reading more complicated texts. This included full speeches from Cicero talking about the Catilinarian conspiracy, and letters from Caesar—things that we didn't really have time for the previous year. Between the stories, our teacher also sprinkled many details, such as how Romans would travel. This allowed me to get a real sense of what Ancient Rome was like and gave me a basic knowledge of Latin culture. Learning the language really did unlock its culture, making the whole experience so much more interesting.

The hard side of Latin still poses many challenges to me, even today. Now, enrolled in my school's Latin AP curriculum, I've never had one day where I walk into my Latin classroom feeling fully prepared. For example, every day for half a year, we would sight-read passages and translate them—and even after all that time, my translation to my teacher still sounds like this:

"Uhh ... Cicero stated ... that ... uhhh ... having been alerted to ... this ... what does this word mean?"

Latin is the only language class where I can spend forty-five minutes completely lost in a two-thousand-year-old sentence. But as frustrating as this sounds, I also don't want to leave. Beneath all the grammatical struggles is a culture just as rich as that of Spanish or Chinese. Maybe it goes back to my early interest in Percy Jackson, but whether it be Roman mythology or Aeneas' journey across the Mediterranean sea, anything in Latin that isn't about grammar intrigues me.

So, while Latin is the most demanding class I've ever taken, I also believe that the fun and cultural side of the language makes struggles worthwhile. Though my journey with Latin is still ongoing, it has already taken me through plenty of twists and turns—and I'm excited to see where it leads next.

While the hard side of Latin still poses many challenges—that might be the hardest of all languages—I know that there will be many more to come. I also believe that the fun and cultural side of the language will balance the struggles I'll face in the future, turning my experience into something more enjoyable. Though short, this journey has definitely had many twists and turns. I'm excited to see what else is in store.

Japanese

新しい言語は新しい人生です

A new language is a new life. — *Anonymous*

After I learned Latin, my fourth language, I thought that that was it. There would be no new paths along my journey of language learning. Four languages was more than enough. Maybe even a little too much.

Luckily enough, I had the chance to stop by Japan in 2023.

For me, Japan had always been somewhere on my bucket list, a place I'd long wanted to visit. From the pictures I saw of Mt. Fuji standing tall over the city of Tokyo to the cyberpunk neon lights around the city, from the renowned foods like ramen and sushi to cherry blossoms and red gates—and that was just the start. There was also anime, TV shows like *Pokemon* ... I could probably go on and on for hours.

But as you may have guessed, I fell in love with Japanese culture through the internet. So, when I learned that I would be traveling there, I wanted to see as much of this fascinating culture in person as I could. I didn't want to only enjoy the sights, the food, and the culture, I wanted to become immersed in it. I had learned from other places and past journeys that the best way to fully experience a culture is total immersion. That meant not just famous sites and famous foods but also the quiet yet bustling atmosphere at night—and more. From prior experience, I'd learned that the best way to travel was to take a deep dive into the culture of the place, and one of the best ways to do that was to learn the local language, just as I learned with Cancun and China.

So, you guessed it, I started to learn Japanese.

This time, however, it was different from all the previous I learned a language. Previous times I had someone there to support me. For example, with Chinese, Latin, and Spanish, I had the help of teachers, and for English and Chinese, I had the help of those always around me, my family and friends. However, for Japanese, it was just me. I had no one to lean on for support, and at first this made me hesitant to learn. But then, there would be all the good memories I would make in Japan if I did indeed learn at least some of the language. Plus, I always wanted to learn another Asian language—especially Japanese. Quite honestly, the characters looked cool, and it would allow me to understand anime and manga better.

So, I started to study Japanese on my own, out of my own interest and motivation. The best way, in my experience, was to use Duolingo, an online language learning app that guides you in self-study. It's a bit like a video game, where you progress through each level in order to reach further levels and simultaneously improve at the language. So I created an account and started learning the basics, including simple words like こんにちわ (hello) and お茶 (green tea), and the Japanese alphabets (hiragana and katakana). By the end of the first few weeks, I felt fairly successful. I felt that the initial aspects of the language were not difficult to pick up, and it was fun doing a lesson or two a day. In addition, the daily goals that the app automatically sets for you motivated me to learn more. Above all else, the language felt… easy. There weren't the struggles or challenges I was used to facing. Maybe it was because of how the lessons were organized, maybe it was because I only spent 15 minutes on it a day, but the process felt surprisingly easy.

After around half a year of self-studying Japanese on Duolingo, it

was time for our trip to Japan. I felt ready. I had practiced around 15 minutes almost every day, only missing a few days because I had other things to do, so I was consistent.

Although I only spent a little time on it each day, it added up, and soon I had learnt a lot—basic phrases, how to order food, and more. I felt confident in my ability. So, I took my half a year of admittedly underwhelming experience and boarded the flight to Tokyo, Japan.

When we landed, I immediately felt like I was in another universe (again)—just like how I felt when I landed in China or Mexico. But Japan was in a league of its own. The soaring modern skyscrapers, the neon Japanese characters floating around me—some I recognized, some I didn't—and the vibe of the city at night. That's what made Tokyo such a unique city at first sight; it felt both futuristic and culturally unique. It wasn't just the sights, either. There were the modern details, like robot servers, high-tech ordering devices, and an atmosphere that made it feel like I had entered a new dimension. Maybe it was because, in the past, Japan had always attempted to preserve its own culture—like I learned in history class. Maybe that was what made its culture so unique.

Soon after we landed, I had my first test in Japanese. We arrived quite late, so my family and I were planning to eat some conveyor belt sushi outside of our hotel. To get us seated and to order, I would most likely have to use some Japanese. But when we walked in, and

the Japanese server greeted us in Japanese, my mind went blank. What was he saying? Why was he speaking so fast? I was able to guess how to greet him back, saying こにちは (hello), because that was the only word of his that I recognized. And that was just about all the Japanese I used in that restaurant. I couldn't recognize many of the items on the menu by reading, so I had to rely on the pictures. I mostly pointed when ordering my food—I wasn't confident enough to engage in a conversation. I didn't know the words, and I felt embarrassed speaking Japanese with a very bad accent to them. The food was great, yet the fact that I was once again not able to engage in conversation in a foreign language left me quite disappointed.

For the rest of the trip I felt the same way: good enough to know a word or two but definitely not good enough to talk to someone. This goes back to "applying what you learned in a real-world situation."

All the time, all the practice I put in—I'd neglected that if I only practiced on my phone then I'd undoubtedly feel uncomfortable communicating with a real person.

So, after I came back from Japan, I did what I thought would help me. I got a Japanese teacher.

My teacher had been a Japanese teacher in Japan, where she usually taught foreigners who had immigrated there. My mom had a friend who knew her—when she brought up that I was learning Japanese, the friend introduced the teacher.

In our first lesson, she introduced herself in English and talked to me a little about my journey in Japanese. Then, we tried to have a conversation.

"How old are you?"

What? I didn't understand her at all—and I couldn't respond at all. All I heard was the word "eat." Scrambling, I pulled out the Duolingo app on my phone to see if I could use it. I couldn't. All I could say was "fifteen" in English, because I didn't know any Japanese numbers over ten. I could tell by her tone that she was disappointed.

That awkward conversation—or, her talking while I tried to respond—would go on for around twenty more minutes. After we finished, she told me what I needed to do. I was completely embarrassed. Not because I didn't know half of what she said but that I failed to recognize how using only Duolingo wasn't enough to build a solid foundation in Japanese. Every time I studied a new foreign language I learned the importance of actually applying it in a real context—and every time afterward I would fail to recognize this lesson, over and over. That was why I felt so embarrassed and frustrated.

So, to fix my mistake, each week, or whenever I was available, we would have a casual lesson based around a conversation. We started with the Japanese alphabets, hiragana and katakana. Even though I knew some of these characters already, this extra practice helped me memorize most of the hiragana characters. Katakana, however, was another story. Whether I felt too lazy to memorize another alphabet or because it was too hard, I didn't fully memorize it until an important Japanese test I would end up taking (yes, that happened). It just goes to show how hard a language Japanese really was. Previously, I always thought Latin had the hardest grammar, but it paled in comparison to Japanese grammar. The main focus of Japanese grammar is verbs, as its language system involves many tenses of verbs, some I had never even seen before (the "masu" form, the plain form, the "-te" form…). They all had to be memorized. Along with them were the rules about how to use those verbs and what context to use them in.

So, I struggled. A lot. It was hard and often overwhelming to memorize all of those forms in all of their tenses, and my teacher would often correct me—sometimes ten times in a class. She would also force me to formulate sentences, and oftentimes I would fail.

At one point, the classes got unbearably hard. I felt so embarrassed and lost all motivation. I wanted to quit, more so than with any other language. In those languages, I had family, friends, and classmates to support me. For Japanese, it was just me.

One night, I talked with my mom about it. She said: "If you want motivation, set a goal for yourself."

I asked myself, what goal? Go back to Japan again? I don't have time for that. Read anime or manga in Japanese? I don't even really like them anymore. Then I thought of something, something at the time I wished I hadn't thought of. Looking back, though, I'm glad I did. A test.

The National Japanese Exam (JSE) was available to students who want to learn Japanese in the US. Maybe, just maybe, if I signed up—the test would keep me motivated.

So, as time went on, with motivation stemming from my competitive side (of course I wanted a good score), I started to take the classes more seriously. Soon, I was improving. My teacher seemed shocked by how much I begun to remember. Over time, I learned the basic grammar and could formulate some simple sentences. From there, I mastered the more complicated verb forms—which make up ninety percent of all the Japanese grammar. Finally, I learned more complicated sentences, like "I cannot go to China because I am traveling elsewhere" and "smoking is not permitted here."

With knowledge of these basic elements, I was able—just like with the other languages I learned—to unlock the culture and other aspects, like holidays, time words (months, numbers, etc.), and foods.

It felt a bit like leveling up in a video game where, after unlocking basic traits, you can use more advanced abilities. Before, I knew how cool Japanese culture was—but I only knew about cyberpunk cities and good food. It was from my classes that I was truly able to experience the uniqueness of the culture. I learned that the culture wasn't just the cyberpunk cities and the good food, it was also the snowy peaks of Hokkaido, the cherry blossoms, and Mt. Fuji. It was tatami mats, small traditional houses, and how modern everything was—even little details like the toilets and the vending machines. Although it seemed like a language class, it allowed me to immerse myself in the language and world of Japan.

Now, about that test.

Thanks to the practice I put in, and thanks to my teacher's help, I was able to excel on the test, receiving the Gold award for those who scored ninety or above. All I'll say is I probably would have quit Japanese if I didn't set a goal for myself. It motivated me to go on, drove me to learn the language, and induced me to immerse myself within Japanese culture. And I'm glad I did, because what I got made the grueling process well worth it.

And, in the summer of 2025, after studying Japanese for around a year, I found myself on another flight back to Japan, this time to Kyoto and Osaka. This time, my parents and I set the same goal: I would use more Japanese. I had spent so long learning Japanese, often feeling quite uncomfortable—I wanted to prove that all the time wasn't in vain.

At first, I could tell that the effort paid off. Although vocabulary still proved to be a struggle (like it is with any other language), I could read way more. Signs that once looked like cryptic symbols now carried meaning. The airport announcements, the chatter of shop clerks, even the muffled voices on train platforms—they were all no longer just noise. I could catch phrases, sometimes full sentences. It was like pieces of a puzzle clicking into place, and at this point, I thought to myself: My hard work was worth it. I'm getting better.

So, I got better at reading and understanding. That was the good news. Then I was thrown into a conversation, and reality hit. My speaking skills, unfortunately, never improved. Throughout the trip, I once again felt myself struggling with speaking. Every time a cashier asked if I wanted a bag, or a waiter confirmed my order, my throat tightened. The words were there, somewhere, rattling around in my mind, but my mouth refused to cooperate. It wasn't just a lack of vocabulary—it was fear. Fear of sounding like a child, fear of the inevitable pause while I scrambled for the right particle, fear of the polite but unmistakable flicker of confusion in the listener's eyes. Instead, I defaulted to nods, gestures, or worse—English. And each time, I walked away kicking myself. Why couldn't I just say it? The words formed in my brain, but my vocal cords just didn't have the courage or energy needed to articulate them into reality.

If my improved reading and writing skills had made my confidence grow, this quickly made my confidence vanish and gave me a feeling that any progress I had made disappeared. So I went back to my hotel and thought about it. After a while, I realized that I'd been here before. Not just in Japan but years earlier, stumbling through Spanish in

Mexico. Back then, I'd assumed fluency would come quickly if I just memorized enough words. But it wasn't until high school, seven years later, that I finally stopped overthinking every sentence.

Japanese was no different. The gap between knowing a language and using it wasn't a flaw in my effort—it was a universal wall every learner hits. And the only way past it was time, patience, and the humility to sound foolish along the way.

So even though I still felt like I had a mouth full of glue, I learned that all I needed was time and consistency to shake the feeling. And slowly but surely, I started. I tried to speak a few words, even if they were simple thank yous or please. Although that might seem quite easy, these are the small steps that you take to improve, and eventually master, a language. Obviously, my Japanese learning journey has only just begun, and quite honestly I might have made it seem quite harsh and difficult. But as hard as it is, I know that there is much more to learn, and I'm excited to see what my fifth language has in store.

Language Learning Tips

So, that's my story—the highs, lows, jokes, and embarrassments. Of course, my journey is far from over. But there is also another reason I wrote this book. It wasn't to brag about how many languages I've learned but to inspire you to begin your own journey. By starting with just one language, believe me, you can open the door to a more vivid, colorful, and meaningful life. It is like unlocking a new ability (for those of you who are video game players), and you begin to see and experience the world in different ways. I won't pretend it's easy. Learning a language is challenging. Just look at how many times I struggled, failed, or did something funny. But those are part of the process. With that in mind, I've put together a few tips from my own experiences and hope they can help a little bit for your journey.

Tip 1: Consistency Matters

When it comes to learning a language, there is no doubt that being consistent is the best way to improve. It is not about how much you do in one day; it is about what you do every day. For example, if you practiced 100 vocabulary words every single week, but for one day only, you might improve quickly at first, but you're also more likely to forget what you learned. On the other hand, if you were to practice only thirty-five to forty vocabulary words a week, but you stuck with five words each day and reviewed them consistently, you would remember them much more effectively over time. This is also supported by the concept of the "memory curve," which suggests that without review, people forget around seventy percent of what they learn within a day. That's why consistency matters.

There were days when I didn't feel motivated, especially on the freezing cold Sunday mornings at Chinese school.

But I still showed up.

Over time, whether memorizing five words a day, or talking in the language for fifteen minutes a day, those small but consistent efforts would pay off. Learning a language isn't about the intensity; it is the consistency. Even just a few minutes each day make a bigger difference than you think.

Tip 2: Don't Try to Figure Everything Out Alone

When you are learning a language, there is no doubt that you will encounter difficulties and challenges. But that doesn't mean that you have to overcome them by yourself.

At one point, when I was struggling the most with English in sixth grade, I thought I could figure everything out on my own. I didn't ask for help, and I ended up falling further behind. When I was learning Spanish, I reached out to my teacher, and it made a huge difference.

There are many resources available, such as online dictionaries or online lectures, but the best resource is the people around you. That could be your parents, your teacher, or your peers. As long as you are willing to ask, you can always find someone who can help you.

Most of the time, people are more supportive than you expect. Many even think it's really cool to speak another language. They won't mind if you ask for a little extra help.

Language learning isn't something you have to do alone. In fact, it's something that becomes much easier, and much more enjoyable, when you learn with others.

Tip 3: Use it, Don't Just Study it

For a long time, I thought that knowing vocabulary and grammar meant I knew the language. But I was wrong, and it was proved again and again on my trips to China, Mexico, Spain, and Japan. I could recognize some words, but I couldn't have a simple conversation. It was only when I started using the language that things began to change.

One of the ways I improved was through immersion in everyday life. For a few years, watching *Running Man* (奔跑吧) in Chinese became my favorite weekend family time. At first, my sister and I were mainly attracted by the actions in their games and could only catch a few words here and there. But over time, we began to understand their conversations, and even some subtle jokes.

Classroom and textbook experiences are not enough on their own, and you need to find opportunities to use what you learned in a real-world situation. Try having simple conversations around daily life—ordering food or just asking about the weather. The more you use it, the more natural it becomes.

If you have the chance, immerse yourself as much as possible. Try the country's food, listen to the music, watch the shows, and engage in their traditions. You will not just improve your language skills, but you will also discover the deeper layers of what a language can offer.

Tip 4: Don't Be Afraid to Sound Foolish

When I was in Japan, I didn't want to speak because I was afraid of making mistakes and sounding like a child. I remember standing at one of the most popular takoyaki stands in Osaka, trying to order for my sister and me but hesitating because I wasn't sure if I was saying it correctly. Even when I knew the words, I second-guessed myself.

What if I pronounced it wrong? What if they didn't understand me?

That's exactly what learning a language looks like. You will hesitate. But that's okay.

I've had moments when I said something slightly off and got a confused look—but those were also the moments I learned the fastest. Just like how I still remember that first successful order of takoyaki and how delicious it was.

If you're willing to sound a little foolish, you're giving yourself a chance to get better.

Tip 5: Set Goals, and Stick to Them

Along the way, I realized that setting goals can make the process of learning a language much more manageable. It motivates you and gives you a sense of accomplishment and pleasure when you achieve it.

Learning a language can be overwhelming, with so many things to master. But if you break it into smaller steps, the process becomes much easier. Who doesn't love the happiness you get from achieving a goal you set for yourself? Even just something as small as keeping a daily Duolingo streak with the little green bird.

Of course, there will be times when you feel like giving up or changing your goal—and all you need to do is try to stick with it.

Learning a language isn't about doing everything at once. Each small step counts.

Tip 6: Let Curiosity Drive You and Have Fun!

Finally, and perhaps most importantly, have fun. Learning a language isn't meant to be dull or boring. It is meant to be fun and interesting! You get to explore aspects of a completely new realm, filled with fascinating things. So don't treat the learning process like torture.

For me, it was the curiosity that kept me going. My trip to China inspired me to take on one of the most challenging languages in the world, while Percy Jackson also led me to Latin. The journey is still ongoing, and I enjoyed every part of it.

Don't focus only on the difficult parts like memorizing vocabulary or practicing conjugations. Embrace the experience and let curiosity guide you—the new things, the new people, and the new ways you'll begin to see the world.

If you're curious, learning a language doesn't feel like a task. It feels like exploration.

Conclusion

So, that's where my journey stands for now. Starting as a child who was just learning the basics of English and growing into a high schooler juggling five languages, my journey has been a whirlwind. From grueling challenges to exciting moments, from the hours spent memorizing parts of speech to the days spent exploring different cultures, it has been one of the most meaningful experiences of my life.

For me, learning a language has always felt different from learning anything else. In subjects like math or science, you learn the concepts and formulas and how to apply them. But language goes beyond that. There is something deeper. That's something no other subject can offer, and that's why I have always loved studying languages, even when others found them challenging or boring.

Looking back, my decision to start learning Chinese wasn't just about learning words. It was what started me on this journey of immersion. To this day, I believe that it might have been the best decision I ever made.

Every language I've learned has given me a new lens—a new way of seeing the world. From Chinese to Spanish, from Latin to Japanese, each language didn't just add to what I knew—it changed how I saw everything around me.

Of course, my journey is far from over. If you choose to start your own journey like me, even with just one language, you'll begin to see a new world.

And once you see the world through a new lens, it's impossible to go back.

Acknowledgments

This book would not have been possible without the support of many people who guided and encouraged me along the way.

First and foremost, I would like to thank my grandparents, who introduced me to Chinese and helped me take my first steps on this journey. Their presence inspired me to explore my heritage more deeply and to connect with the world around me.

I am grateful to my parents, who supported me through every step of this journey. Not every parent encourages their child to pursue five languages for over ten years, and I am thankful that they were always there for me.

Special thanks to my sister, Irena Mao, who is my Duolingo partner and also collaborated with me on the illustrations for this book.

I am also deeply grateful to my teachers and classmates for supporting me in learning languages, especially those who patiently helped me through challenges and encouraged me to never give up.

Finally, thank you to everyone who has been part of this experience—family, friends, and the communities I've encountered across languages and cultures. Big or small, every step has led me to who I am today.

Felix Mao is a student at Rye Country Day School in Rye, New York, with a passion for languages, and linguistics. Spanning five languages, his journey has been full of twists and turns, including cultural experiences, awkward conversations, and "aha" moments along the way.

Felix has demonstrated notable achievement across diverse language families, earning national Gold Medals in Latin, Spanish, and Japanese, and a perfect score on the AP Chinese exam. He is also a published researcher in corpus and computational linguistics, with work presented at international conferences and published in peer-reviewed proceedings.

Beyond languages, Felix explores how artificial intelligence and machine learning can reshape communication in ways similar to human language. He is also an athlete and artist who enjoys playing baseball and basketball, creating art, and spending time with family and friends.

In *Changing Lens*, Felix invites readers to see the world through perspectives shaped by different languages and cultures.